04/83

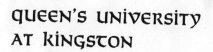

The Secret Life of
HARDWARE

The Secret Life of

HARDWARE

A Science Experiment Book

Vicki Cobb

illustrated by Bill Morrison

J.B. LIPPINCOTT   NEW YORK

For my son, Josh,
who loves to unlock secrets
of the mechanical

Library of Congress Cataloging in Publication Data

Cobb, Vicki.
　The secret life of hardware.

　Summary: Examines the inventory of a hardware
store from the tools to glues and suggests experiments
which demonstrate the scientific principles
and legends behind these items.
　1. Hardware—Juvenile literature.　[1. Hardware.
2. Experiments]　I. Morrison, Bill, 1935–　ill.
II. Title.
TS400.C63 1982　　　670　　　81–48607
ISBN 0–397–31999–1　　　AACR2
ISBN 0–397–32000–0 (lib. bdg.)

1　2　3　4　5　6　7　8　9　10
First Edition

Contents

1. THE STORIES THEY COULD TELL . . . 1

2. SURFACE STUFF: CLEANERS, POLISHES, WAXES 4

   Hard-Surface Cleaners 6 *Photochemistry 13*
   Wetting Agents 8 *Other Metals 16*
   Cleaning Metal Surfaces 10 *Waxes 17*

3. PAINTS 21

   Paint Films 23 *Pigments 27*
   Drying Oils 25 *Mix Your Own Paints 28*

4. CONNECTORS 31

   The Anatomy of a Rope 33 *Glue 40*
   Laying a Rope 34 *Make Your Own Glue 41*
   Natural Plant Cordage 36 *Tapes 44*
   Fiber Flame Test 38

5. TOOLS: SIMPLE MACHINES 46

   The Claw Hammer 49 *Screws 60*
   The Saw 55 *Turning Tools 63*
   Nails, Tacks, Chisels,
     and Other Wedges 58

6. ELECTRICITY 66

   Charges 67 *Batteries 75*
   Make a Charge Detector 69 *Circuits 78*
   Make a Current Detector 72 *Resistance 81*

   INDEX 85

1. The Stories They Could Tell . . .

What if all the items in a hardware store could talk. What stories would they tell? How they were invented? How they got to be so good at the jobs they do? I'll bet you can't imagine some of their tales. The lowly American nail might brag of the time when metal nails were a measure of a person's wealth. That was when the West was expanding. Settlers with nails could build homes more quickly than settlers without them, who had to fashion wooden pegs. Thus nails gave an advantage to people staking claims on the frontier. Paint might recall a brown shade called "mummy" that appeared on the market in Europe for a short time until it was revealed that it was indeed made from ground-up mummies. Stories like these, of wealth and scandal, are not the only little-known facts behind hardware.

Even more fascinating is how modern hand tools, coatings, glues, and electrical equipment do what they do. Suppose you had a special job to do, like hanging a door, or putting two pieces of wood together, or stretching some fabric over a frame, and that there were no tools. Do you think you could invent something to do the job? What if you had to start from scratch and make your own glue? Would you know where to begin? And what about all those household chemicals that remove dirt, or tarnish, or wax, or paint, or almost any sort of substance that might wind up on every type of surface. Do you have any idea what they are made of?

Hardware is just some of that commonplace yet crucial stuff that most of us take for granted. But stop. Think. Imagine all the thought and experimenting that must have gone into a modern hardware store inventory to make it what it is. These stories are what I call "the secret life of hardware." Most people don't know much about them.

In this book you'll explore a lot of seldom-asked questions. What are the unique scientific principles that enable different items from the hardware store to do their jobs? How can you create your own, at home, from scratch? What can be learned about physics, and chemistry, and history, and human creativity from the hardware store? We ask these questions and more in each chapter. You can discover the answers yourself by doing experiments and getting involved with hardware in ways you never dreamed possible.

Here's how to use this book. You can, first of all, simply read it as you might read any book of nonfiction. I've included some interesting background on the history of technology behind modern products, always stressing the principles without getting bogged down in details. Secondly, you can use this book as a how-to guide. There are many procedures for experiments. These procedures work. I've checked them all out in my home laboratory. But you may think of another way to do them. Bravo! No book should ever be the final word for any creative experimenter. Trust your own hunches. Maybe *you* will be the one to build the better mousetrap! Lots of stuff in the modern hardware store are the products of individual inventors. And they are still changing because of the work by present inventors and scientists. Follow up your own results. Perhaps the U.S. Patent Office will hear from you. Think of this book as a beginning.

Hardware can be the start of a scientific adventure. Discover its secret life!

2. Surface Stuff: Cleaners, Polishes, Waxes

The earliest household cleaner was probably water and sand, for rubbing. Three hundred years ago, in colonial America, the chief cleaners for floors and dishes were sand, strong homemade soap, and elbow grease—hard rubbing, in case you never heard the term. Today there is a large industry supported by the desire on the part of consumers to have their homes clean and shining. Hardware stores all have a section for household cleaners, a baffling array of products ranging from general "all-purpose" types to specialists for polishing metals, making glass sparkle, or cleaning ovens. Instead of sand, modern cleaners contain finely ground pumice (a volcanic rock) or rottenstone. These are abrasives that, like sand, clean by rubbing off some surface along with the dirt. Harsh soaps have been replaced by a number of different chemicals that are identified by their technical names: anionic surfactants, sodium citrate, sodium carbonate, calcium carbonate, and ammonia, to name a few.

Much of cleaning depends on getting dirt loose from a surface so that it can be flushed away with water. But the soiled surfaces of metals require different treatment. Metal tarnish is the result of a chemical reaction between a metal and some chemical in the air. In order to remove the tarnish, another chemical reaction must take place. The reaction that takes place depends on the metal, the tarnish, and the chemical in the metal polish. Needless to say, there are some fascinating chemical reactions in metal polishing.

And finally, when a surface is bright and clean, it's time to protect it and shine it up with wax. Waxes are a class of chemicals that have unusual properties for repelling water and buffing to a shine.

Cleaners, polishes, and waxes are for surfaces. But you can look

deeper into the history and the chemistry behind them in this chapter.

Hard-Surface Cleaners

Water is undoubtedly the cheapest and most abundant cleaner around. Unfortunately, it is not the most efficient. Although it is called the "universal solvent" because more chemicals dissolve in water than in any other liquid, there is a large class of compounds that simply don't mix at all with water: greases and oils. When dirt adheres to grease that adheres to surfaces, something besides water is called for.

Soaps and detergents are substances that mix with both greases and water. When oil, water, and soap are mixed together, soap molecules become arranged between water and fat molecules, held in a suspension called an *emulsion*. Although the emulsion is often temporary, it lasts long enough to flush away the grease along with the dirt.

The cleaning solutions sold in hardware stores are called "hard-surface" soaps and detergents, as opposed to the kind of detergents used in washing machines.

Materials and Equipment

– small, slim olive jars with lids, as many as you can collect
  (Olive jars are a good substitute for test tubes.   However, if
  you have access to test tubes, use them instead.)
– measuring cup
– measuring spoons
– salad oil

– assortment of soaps: liquid, soap flakes, detergents, etc.
– assortment of hard-surface cleaners: Fantastik, Mr. Clean, Windex, etc.
– clock
– pencil and paper

Procedure

Put a quarter cup of cold water in each jar. Add one tablespoon of salad oil to each jar. Put the lid on one jar containing oil and water. This will be the "control" in your experiment. (A control has all of the elements of an experiment *except* the one you are changing.) Add one teaspoon of soap or hard-surface cleaner to each of the other jars. Label each jar so you know which cleaner you have added. Shake the jar containing oil and water hard about five times. Using the second hand on a clock, see how long it takes to separate into two clear separate layers of oil and water. I found that my sample separated in about forty-five seconds.

Now shake a jar containing one of your cleaning solutions five times. Measure the time it takes to separate into two separate layers. Repeat for each setup of oil, water, and cleaner.

Observations and Suggestions

The longer it takes for the oil and water to separate into two layers, the better the emulsifier. The better the emulsion, the more time you have to rinse away dirt. I found that liquid soap was better than hard-surface cleaners. Some brands were faster than others, also. Try powdered cleaners. Dissolve a small amount in water before you add a teaspoon to the oil-water mixture. Do an experiment to see how water temperature affects the emulsification.

Wetting Agents

In order for any cleaning solution to have an effect, it must come into intimate contact with the surface it is applied to. It must *wet* the surface. Water molecules wet a surface when they are more attracted to the surface molecules than they are to each other. The attraction water molecules have for each other is easiest to observe where water molecules pull together at the surface to form a kind of skin. You can see such a skin of *surface tension* as a drop forms at the end of a faucet. All liquids have surface tension, and you can easily compare different liquids by putting equal-sized drops on waxed paper and comparing the height of the drops. Some will be flatter drops than others.

Hard-surface cleaners all contain wetting agents called *surfactants.* The cleaning solution industry has developed a variety of surfactants. Do an experiment to compare their ability as wetting agents.

Materials and Equipment

- brown paper bag
- scissors
- pencil
- salad oil
- paper towel
- hair dryer (optional)
- a selection of hard-surface cleaners from under
  your sink: for general cleaning,
  glass, woodwork, floors, etc.
- shallow dishes

– straws, one for each kind of cleaner

– measuring spoons

Procedure

Cut pieces of brown paper bag about two inches square. With the pencil, label each one for a cleaning solution you intend to test. Label one "control." Spread about half a teaspoon of salad oil on each piece of paper. The salad oil will sink into the paper. Spread it evenly, and wipe up any excess with paper toweling.

Pour a sample of the cleaning solutions, each in its own shallow dish. Dip the oil-coated paper labeled for a cleaner in that solution. Let the cleaning solution dry on the paper. Use a hair dryer to speed up the drying process if you wish. After all the pieces of oiled paper have been coated with a cleaning solution and dried, you are ready to do your experiment. Note: do not treat the paper labeled "control" with any cleaning solution.

Put a drop of water on each piece of paper. To make sure that each piece of paper gets the same size drop, dip a straw into a glass of water. A small amount will remain in the end of the straw when you lift it out. Gently blow into the straw so that the drop lands on the paper. You can compare the wetting ability of the different surfactants by the curve of the drop of water. Water will not wet an oiled surface, and a drop pulls together to create a high, rounded shape. The rounder the drop, the less the surface is being wet. The best surfactants will cause the drop of water to spread through the paper.

Observations and Suggestions

In my experiments, I found that a window cleaner had the least wetting ability for this particular test, while a household general cleaner was the best. Water was the roundest on the oiled but untreated control.

If you wish, you can make a survey of different hard-surface cleaners for their emulsifying ability and wetting ability. Use the procedure in the previous experiment to determine emulsifying ability, and this procedure for measuring wetting ability. Are cleaners with good surfactants also good emulsifiers? Experiment and find out.

Cleaning Metal Surfaces

In every hardware store there is a section devoted to metal polishes. The purpose of these polishes is to remove tarnish from the surface of silver, copper, pewter, or brass. Tarnish is not just a dirty surface. Tarnish is a discoloring due to a chemical reaction of the metal with substances in the air. Most metal polishes are partly chemical reaction with the tarnish and partly a mild abrasive that gently rubs off the surface of the metals. Do the following series of experiments to explore some of the chemistry behind metals.

Polishing Silver

Silver is a lustrous white metal that is second to gold in value among the precious metals. Pure silver is too soft to be useful, so a small amount of copper is mixed in when it is molten, to form sterling silver. The term "sterling" comes from the time in the middle ages when it was used for the English penny. The copper-silver proportions for sterling silver became the standard mixture for British coins.

Silver tarnish is a compound of silver and sulfur, called silver sulfide. Any substance that contains sulfur will sooner or later tarnish silver. The air contains minute amounts of sulfur dioxide, a gas that smells like rotten eggs. The amount is so small that we hardly ever notice it. You can do an experiment to see the effect of different sulfur-containing materials on polished silver. You will need silver or silver-plated teaspoons. Polish them with any silver polish.

All of the following materials contain sulfur. Put samples on each teaspoon and see how long it takes to develop the black coating of silver sulfide.

– mustard
– molasses
– egg white
– mayonnaise
– cooked vegetable water from cabbage, onions, turnip, cauliflower, or kale (The vegetables should be boiled twenty minutes to develop the sulfur. Keep the pot covered to keep the sulfur compounds from boiling off, and let the water cool with the cover on.)
– crushed garlic (Crushing releases the sulfur compounds.)
– rubber (A rubber band around silver should produce a tarnished area.)

You can also experiment with different kinds of tarnish removers. Compare different kinds of commercial cleaners. There are basically two kinds. Pastes or creams contain a mild soap along with a very fine abrasive material. There is no chemical reaction in the silver. They remove the tarnish by rubbing it off with the abrasive, which is so fine it doesn't harm the silver.

Dip polishes contain a strong acid that removes tarnish chemically.

You can also clean silver electrically:

Materials and Equipment

– a stainless steel or enamel saucepan
– aluminum foil
– baking soda
– salt
– measuring spoon
– tarnished silver

Procedure

Cover the inside of the saucepan with aluminum foil, shiny side up. Put in four cups of water, one tablespoon of baking soda, and one teaspoon of salt. Bring the mixture to a boil, and slip in the tarnished silver. The silver must be touching the foil. Watch as the tarnish disappears. Let the mixture boil slowly as it works on the silver. If you have a heavily tarnished piece, you may have to boil it at least fifteen minutes. Fish out the silver with tongs, or let it cool in the pan before you remove it. Rinse the silver and wipe it dry. Take a close look at the aluminum foil in the pan.

Observations and Suggestions

How does the used foil compare with fresh foil? The aluminum appears tarnished because it is. Aluminum is a more chemically active metal than silver. That is, under the proper circumstances sulfur molecules will combine with aluminum rather than with silver. In this experiment you set up the proper circumstances. Here's how:

The hot solution of baking soda breaks up the silver sulfide tarnish into electrically charged atoms or ions of silver and sulfur. The silver ions stay on the surface of the silver. But the sulfur ions are carried through the solution (which is called an electrolyte because it will carry an electric current) to the surface of the aluminum. There, the sulfur ions react chemically with the aluminum to form aluminum sulfide. (Learn more about electrolytes and electricity in Chapter 6.)

Photochemistry

Silver is extremely important in the development of modern photography. The day the secret of photography was announced was a momentous one.

On August 19, 1839, an overflow crowd impatiently waited for news outside the French Academy of Sciences. Inside, two scientists, Joseph Niepce and Louis Daguerre, were to make public a secret process for making permanent pictures with sunlight. For many, it was the scientific revelation of the century, and rumors flew through the restless crowd. One man said, "You use a kind of tar." Another said, "No, I'm sure it's nitric acid." Finally, a nervous little man appeared at the top steps. The crowd surged forward. "Silver, iodine, and mercury," he whispered. Those three elements and the way they were used were the beginning of modern photography.

Photography is based on the reaction of certain silver compounds with light. As long as you have the silver polish out, see if you can get some photochemical reactions. You can do it without the mercury. See for yourself.

Materials and Equipment

- a very tarnished piece of silver or silver plate
- paste or cream silver polish
- a piece of clean cotton cloth, about two inches square
- two glasses
- a funnel
- coffee filter paper, or paper towel
- chlorine bleach (Note: be careful not to get this on your clothes, or in a cut.)
- plastic wrap
- a flat piece of silver or silver plate
- iodine (from the medicine chest)

Procedure

Moisten the cloth and use a small amount of silver polish to rub off the tarnish. The cloth should get quite black. You have now moved the silver sulfide onto the cloth.

In a dimly lit area, put the cloth in the glass, and pour bleach over it. Stir it so that the black tarnish goes into the liquid and becomes a cloudy, white solution. You have just made silver sulfide react with the chlorine to form silver chloride, a photo-chemical substance.

Working quickly, fold the filter paper in half and then in half again so that you can open it into a cone. Place the open cone into the funnel. Put the end of the funnel in the empty glass, and pour the silver chloride mixture into the filter paper. After the liquid has finished dripping, remove the filter paper. Unfold it carefully, and cover the silver chloride with clear plastic wrap. You don't want it to dry out too quickly. Cover a part of the film of silver chloride with a coin, and place it in direct sunlight. After about twenty minutes, lift the coin to see if you have gotten a silhouette.

Early photographers used plates of silver that had been treated chemically to form light-sensitive surfaces. You can do the same.

Polish the flat piece of silver. In dim light, flood the surface with iodine. Rinse. While it is wet, place it in a strong light. Cover a small part with an opaque object. You should get a silhouette within a few minutes.

Observations and Suggestions

In both cases, you'll notice that although you'll get an image, it fades very quickly when the area that was covered is exposed to light. Also, the light-sensitive chemicals must be wet in order to react. Early photographers used "wet plates," which were really silver plates that were treated chemically and were light-sensitive when they were wet. Photography really got off the ground when images recorded on wet plates were treated with chemical "fixatives" that prevented them from darkening. One such early fixative contained ammonia. See if household ammonia poured over the iodine-treated silver can prolong the image.

You can easily restore the silver to its previous luster with silver polish.

Other Metals

Other metals that are commonly used for household items include copper, brass (a mixture of copper and zinc), tin (an element), aluminum (an element), and pewter (a mixture of tin and antimony). To one degree or another, all of these metals tarnish by combining chemically with oxygen in the air. (Stainless steel does not tarnish so we're not considering it here.) Most metal polishes work by a combination of chemistry and a fine abrasive. When the mild acid in the polish comes in contact with the metal oxide, the metal is restored to its uncombined state. Copper becomes red, and brass becomes golden.

You can get commercial polishes for all these metals in your hardware store. Compare their polishing ability with some of these home formulas:

– For copper: a mixture of vinegar and salt
– For brass: vinegar and salt
         – ammonia (A blue color on cloth rubbed on brass indicates the removal of copper. When copper

combines with ammonia chemically, it is blue in
color.)
  – Worcestershire sauce (No kidding! Except it didn't
  work when I tried it. Maybe it will work for you.)
– For tin: rub with a sliced onion
– For pewter: rub with raw cabbage leaves
– For aluminum: boil with grapefruit and orange skins, or boil
  with cream of tartar, from the spice rack

Waxes

Waxes are a group of compounds that are solid at ordinary temperatures, not greasy, do not dissolve in water, and melt at fairly
low temperatures, below the boiling point of water. They may
come from plants, animals, insects, or minerals. They burn and
can be used as fuel. They are extremely useful in all kinds of
products, from packaging cosmetics to textiles to polishes for different surfaces. They have been used for thousands of years. Ancient Persians called wax *mum,* and the word *mumiya* refers to
the specially treated corpse, embalmed with beeswax, that we
call a mummy. You can buy different kinds of wax at the hardware store. Waxes can be buffed to a shine because they are made
up of long molecules. When you rub them, you line up the molecules in the same direction and they reflect light. Different kinds
of waxes are more or less buffable.

Wax protects surfaces because water will not wet it. Put a drop
of water on a piece of waxed paper. See how the drop pulls together into a ball. This shows the surface tension of the water.
The drop will roll around and slide right off the wax. For this

reason, many plant waxes are found on the stems and leaves of plants, especially in tropical climates. Water rolls off the surface without soaking into the plant. This keeps the plant from rotting. Wax on apples does the same job and can be polished to a high gloss.

Organic chemists who study waxes make a note of their different properties. They are particularly interested in the temperature at which a wax melts. This so-called melting point is one way of identifying a wax and determining how pure it is. The purer a wax, the smaller the range of temperature at which it melts. Do an experiment in organic chemistry of your own. You can apply this procedure for measuring melting points that are below the boiling point of water to all kinds of organic substances, including fats.

Materials and Equipment

– a large saucepan (2 quarts)
– six aluminum foil muffin cups

– three plastic teaspoons
– beeswax
– paraffin
– paste floor wax
– thermometer showing temperatures up to the boiling point of
    water (212°F or 100°C), optional

Procedure

Put about two tablespoons of each kind of wax in a muffin cup. Fill the pan half full of water, and float the cups containing wax in it. Put the pan over a flame on the stove. You have created a "hot-water bath," as they say in the lab. Heat the bath until all the wax in each of the cups is completely melted.

Working quickly, fill one of the plastic spoons with one sample of melted wax, and pour it into an empty muffin cup. Move the cup around so the melted wax evenly coats the bottom. Repeat with the other two waxes, using a new spoon for each. You want to have a thin, even layer of the same amount of wax in each cup.

Let the three samples cool for at least fifteen minutes. Put fresh cool water in the pan. Set in your three samples floating on top. Put the pan over the burner, with the tip of the thermometer in the water measuring its temperature. Light the burner. Watch very carefully to see which wax melts first. As each sample melts, note the temperature of the water.

Observations and Suggestions

You can repeat this experiment several times to make sure of your results, using the same wax samples. Just let them cool and harden between tests. It is important that you have a very thin, even layer of wax on the bottom of the cup. Done correctly, the complete melting of a wax occurs within a few seconds and within a few degrees of change in temperature. Melting point is considered a physical property of pure materials. The paste floor wax will probably show melting over the longest period of time because it is the least pure of the three samples.

Here are some interesting details on the three kinds of wax: Beeswax comes from honeycombs. It is secreted by wax glands of worker honeybees and is fashioned into the cell of a honeycomb by their jaws. Bees secrete one pound of wax for every eight pounds of honey. Its melting point is 108°–118°F (42–48°C). Paste floor wax's main ingredient is carnauba wax. It is a very hard, brittle, nonsticky wax that can be buffed to a high shine. It comes from the leaves of a Brazilian palm tree. Its melting point is 180° –187°F (82.5°–86°C). Paraffin is a byproduct of the petroleum industry. It is a white, hard, dry solid without any smell or taste, and as such is well suited to being in contact with food. Melted paraffin easily impregnates paper goods for all kinds of packaging material, hence its use on waxed paper. Its melting point is 125° –165°F (40°–60°C).

Since you can use and reuse your wax samples to determine melting points by this method, you can check out other waxes around your house. What kind of wax is used around cheeses? What are candles made of? Shoe polish? Lipstick?

You can also use this procedure to measure the melting points of fats, substances related to oils. Check out butter, margarine, vegetable shortening, bacon grease, etc. Refrigerate the samples to get them good and hard before you run the melting point test.

3. Paints

Cleaning and polishing were not the only way people worked to change surfaces around them. For 20,000 years, from the first colored drawings on the walls of caves to the present day, dramatic changes have been brought about by decorating, coloring, and preserving surfaces with paint. Paint can be defined as a colored liquid that can be applied to a surface, where it becomes a dry film.

Your hardware store offers an enormous selection of paints. There are paints for interiors and exteriors, paints to prevent rust, paints that keep cement from cracking, poisonous paints to keep barnacles from clinging to boats, and nonpoisonous paints for children's furniture. And they come in every shade of every color of the rainbow. You also have a choice of delivery system. Paints can be brushed on, wiped on, sprayed on, rolled on, poured on, or dipped on. The final film can be glossy, flat, or glow in the dark. And finally, you can clean up using a solvent for oil, such as turpentine, or with water.

But no matter what kind of paint you choose, all paint has three basic ingredients. First there is the coloring agent or *pigment.* Pigments, as opposed to dyes, do not dissolve in the solvent. They are tiny particles of colored material that are suspended in the liquid or *vehicle* of the paint and will be the opaque color of the paint film. (Dyes that are also coloring agents do dissolve in the vehicle and stain material. They do not remain on the surface.) The *vehicle,* or liquid suspending the pigment, has two other parts. One part is the *binder* that actually forms the dry film and binds the pigment to the surface. The third ingredient is the *solvent* or thinner that controls the consistency of the paint in its liquid form. It is a fugitive substance, one that evaporates and leaves the others behind.

Never doubt that there are lots of scientists in the paint industry. Modern paints are a direct result of chemists and chemical engineers who have examined the properties of various materials that are suited to becoming a part of an amazing dry film most of us take for granted. In this chapter you can explore some of the physical and chemical properties of paint and its ingredients. Believe me, it's not whitewash.

Paint Films

The object of any paint is the quality of the dry film it becomes. A paint film is extremely thin, anywhere from one one thousandth of an inch to four one-thousandths of an inch thick. Paint protects wood surfaces by slowing down the rate at which water reaches the wood. Most household paints are fairly waterproof. Since the paint films are so thin, it is very important that the paint stick to its surface, and paint chemists spend a great deal of time studying the adhesive bond between paint and various surfaces.

You can do a study of the formation of paint films where the paint does not stick to the surface. The kind of paint you are likely to have around the house forms a film by the process of solvent evaporation. There is a change in the molecular structure of the film as it dries. Some coatings, like shellac, don't go through any additional chemical change when the solvent evaporates. Here's how you can demonstrate this. If you put alcohol on a shellacked surface, the shellac will be dissolved by its solvent. But latex paints, which have water as a solvent, and oil-based paints continue to change after the solvent has evaporated. As a result, the solvent no longer works on the dried paint. The following experiment explores different kinds of paint films.

Materials and Equipment

– plastic covers from coffee or tennis-ball cans
– Vaseline
– plastic straws
– paints and varnishes you have on hand, including shellac, varnish, latex paint, oil-based paint
– paint scraper or razor

Procedure

Clean the plastic tops. You should have one for each kind of coating. Smear a thin layer of Vaseline over one side of each cover. This will make it easy to lift off the dried paint film. Mix all your paint samples thoroughly. It's important.

Dip a clean plastic straw into the paint to a depth of half an inch. Put your finger over the top as you lift it out of the paint can. Let the paint run out of the straw by lifting your finger on to the center of the Vaseline-coated cover. Blow out the remaining paint in the straw. Tilt the cover back and forth to get the paint to spread in a smooth layer. Repeat this procedure for each kind of paint.

Let your samples dry overnight. The next day, peel off your paint films with a paint scraper. You may get only pieces of film, but you will be able to see differences in thickness. Pull on the films. Some kinds will be stronger than others. Fold them. Some will be more flexible than others. If you can get a large enough piece of film, put it on blotting paper. Put a drop of water on the paint. If the water seeps through the film, you will see a spot on the paper.

Observations and Suggestions

Which kind of paint dried fastest? There are three stages to drying: tacky, touch-dried, and "through" dried. Some paints take several months to become through dried. Keep your paint films. See if they change over time. Which films become brittle first?

One of the properties of liquid paint is *viscosity,* or the rate at which it flows. You can compare the viscosity of paints with the following procedure: Spread newspapers to work over. Dip the end of a clean plastic straw in each sample of paint to a depth of one inch. Remove the sample by putting your finger over the end of the straw. Work quickly in collecting your samples. Rest the straw with the end containing the paint on some object so that the paint runs downhill through the straw. See how long it takes for the paint to reach the bottom of the straw and run out. Different kinds of paints will have different viscosities. A low-viscosity paint will form a thinner paint film than a high-viscosity paint. Do your experiments confirm this statement?

Drying Oils

The film in paint is formed by the binder. Most binders are molecules made of long chains of atoms. Repeating units of long chains of molecules are called polymers. In the dried film, polymers form a network that trap pigment particles. Among the most important binders for paint films is a group of chemicals called *drying oils.*

Oils are liquids that leave translucent spots on brown paper, like fats. They come from a variety of plants and animals. The oils from certain plants will become a hard film when exposed to air. These are the drying oils. Some oils, called semidrying, eventually form a soft film. Others will not form a film no matter how long they are exposed to the air, and these are called nondrying.

Do an experiment with oils around your house to see whether they are drying, semidrying, or nondrying. Look for oils among your paint supplies, in the pantry (salad oils), and in the medicine chest.

Materials and Equipment

– pencil and paper
– plastic lids
– plastic straws
– assortment of oils, including linseed, tung, soya, safflower, cottonseed, olive, vegetable, etc.

Procedure

Use a clean straw and plastic lid for each sample. Dip the straw into the oil to a depth of half an inch. Remove the sample by putting your finger over the open end. Put the tip containing the oil over the center of the plastic lid. Lift your finger and let the oil run out. Move the lid around so that the oil spreads evenly. Write the name of the sample on a piece of paper. Set the lid containing the sample near the name you have written on the paper. Repeat the procedure for each kind of oil in your experiment.

Let the oil dry for several days. Check them for drying twice a day. Keep a record of which oils dry first. Some will take a week to dry.

Observations and Suggestions

Oils you get from the paint supplies will undoubtedly prove to be the drying oils. Of these, linseed oil from the seeds of flax plants, which also give us linen cloth, is one of the most important drying oils. When a drying oil dries, it combines chemically with oxygen in the air. This reaction does two things. It makes the dry film chemically different from the oil, so that the solvent can no longer dissolve it. Rub turpentine on dried oil paint and you'll see why paint removers are a different kind of chemical. Second, the addition of oxygen causes the film to expand. If you have a thick layer of linseed oil, the surface of the film will dry long before the underlying oil. The expansion of the dry surface on top of the smaller area of liquid oil will produce wrinkling. The incredibly orderly patterning of the wrinkled surface of linseed oil is proof of the orderliness of the molecular structure of the material. To see this truly remarkable event, repeat the procedure for this experiment, only put a larger sample of linseed oil (dip the straw to a depth of one inch) on the plastic lid.

Pigments

Paint color and opaqueness (shutting off light) are due to pigments. Most pigments are some kind of mineral that has been ground to a fine powder. You can grind your own pigments, which you can use to make your own paint.

Materials and Equipment

- aluminum-foil muffin cups
- hammer handle
- charcoal
- small flowerpot or brick
- colored chalk

Procedure

The mortar and pestle were the ancient means of grinding pigments, but most households are not likely to have them around. You can improvise a pestle with the handle of a hammer or the back of a spoon. Throughout history, black pigment has been some form of carbon. You can crush a piece of charcoal or charred wood. Or you can collect lampblack, pure carbon, by holding a metal spoon over a burning candle. Be sure to check with an adult before you do this. The metal of the spoon absorbs the heat, causing the candle to burn incompletely. Carbon collects as soot on the spoon, and can be scraped off. Lampblack collected this way is already finely divided and doesn't need to be ground.

A brick or a terra-cotta flowerpot is a good source of a red-brown pigment. Break it up into small pieces with a hammer, then grind it with a little water in an aluminum cup.

Colored chalks already have finely divided pigments in them. Commercial chalks are made of plaster of Paris, and when you crush them with a little water, you'll create both a colored pigment and an "extender" pigment. Extender pigments are used in the paint industry to improve the consistency of the paint. They have little coloring value.

Paint a surface with a mixture of pigment and water. What happens when there is no binder present?

Mix Your Own Paints

Now that you have paint binders and pigments, it makes sense to experiment with mixing your own paints. Here's a list of the various things you can use to create your own paint.

Materials and Equipment

– aluminum-foil muffin cups
– paintbrushes
– paper towels
– unpainted wood
– turpentine

Binders

– egg yolk beaten with water (makes egg tempera)
– one tablespoon low-fat cottage cheese mixed with one table-
    spoon warm water and one teaspoon baking soda
– linseed oil

Pigments

– dry powdered graphite (hardware store)
– finely crushed powdered chalk
– finely crushed flowerpot
– finely crushed charcoal
– spices such as paprika, tumeric, curry powder

Procedure

This is an open-ended experiment, where you can try all sorts of combinations to see if you can come up with a paint of your own that really works.

For oil-based paint: Mix finely powdered pigment with a small amount of linseed oil. The consistency should be that of sour cream. Paint on the wooden surface and allow to dry. Clean your brush by dipping it in turpentine and wiping it clean with paper toweling. Oil-based paints are the most durable. They are used for outside surfaces.

For casein paint: Casein is milk protein. Mix a tablespoon of low-fat cottage cheese with a teaspoon of baking powder and a tablespoon of warm water. Let stand for at least one hour, stirring from time to time. The baking soda breaks down the curds into a form that dissolves. Let the mixture stand overnight. It will be ready to use as a binder when it is smooth and clear. Mix in pigment. Add water if necessary to get the right consistency. Paint on the wood. Clean your brush with water. Artists still use casein paint.

For egg tempera: Separate the white from the yolk. Ask the cook in your house to show you how. Beat the egg yolk with a quarter cup of water. Mix with pigment. You'll need two sticks of chalk per egg yolk. Paint on paper. Clean your brush with water. Artists use egg tempera for clear, bright color. It is very tricky to use.

Observations and Suggestions

After your paint samples have dried, rub them with your finger. See if the pigment comes loose. Compare your results with the painting you did in the last experiment with just pigment and water.

Experiment with other materials as binders. Try a solution of unflavored gelatin in three tablespoons of water. Try white glue, and liquid laundry starch.

4. Connectors

Suppose you want to connect several objects for a short period of time and nails or screws won't do it for you. Suppose you want to hoist something two stories. Suppose you want a smooth joint between two surfaces. What are the best solutions to such predicaments? Enter the hardware store, your personal problem-solving center. There you can confront an assortment of ropes, twines, cords, strings, cables, tapes, and glues. They hold the promise for answers to countless questions, many of them yet to be dreamed up.

The catchall term for all the different kinds of long, flexible structures that can be tied in knots is *cordage.* Earliest cordage, perhaps for tying branches together for shelter or hanging meat or leather to dry, was probably made of strips of animal hide or long grass or vines. Modern cordage has come a long, long way. You can find some kind of cordage to meet any particular requirements of strength, flexibility, stretch, durability, and resistance to mildew and rot. Cordage is made of natural vegetable fibers, syn-

thetic materials, glass, or steel. It may be braided or twisted, and it can have a core made of one material covered by a sheath layer of another. There are, however, certain basic principles having to do with cordage that you can explore in this chapter.

Adhesives are another area well developed by hardware manufacturers. Glues have been developed for bonds between porous materials, such as wood, and nonporous, such as china and glass. The secret to adhesives is contact between the glue and a surface. But more on that later.

Tapes, like all the other categories of hardware, do numerous jobs. There are tapes for decoration, repair, insulation, and connections between objects. Most tapes rely on pressure-sensitive adhesives that can be the basis of an experiment. Do the experiments in this chapter and make your own connection with the connectors!

The Anatomy of a Rope

One of the earliest ropes was a lasso, woven by some ancient tribesman to catch a straying animal. It was both strong and flexible. Modern cordage comes in a variety of strengths, thicknesses, and prices, depending on its intended use.

One way of trying to understand something is to take it apart. You can learn a great deal about cordage by taking apart samples of rope, twine, and string. Make a collection of different kinds of cordage. You don't need to buy anything. If you don't have much lying around your house, local merchants may be happy to give you bits and pieces from their packaging materials.

Take a two-inch piece of any cordage. Most cordage has one very obvious property: twist. The twist is in one of two directions. Grasp the cord with each hand. Hold one end firmly with your less favorite hand. Rotate the other end between the thumb and first finger of your favorite hand. If a counterclockwise motion with your right hand unwinds the cord, the cord has been given an S twist. If a clockwise motion unwinds it, the cord has been given a Z twist.

Different kinds of cordage have different amounts of twist. You can see this difference by comparing the number of times you turn over one end of a piece of cord to unwind it. Many cords will separate into strands or *plies* as you unwind them. The most common is three-ply cord, with three strands. Often the strands themselves have been twisted. Check the direction of the twist in the strands. If the cord has an S twist, the ply often has a Z twist.

If you continue to untwist the strands, eventually you'll end up with a single fiber. Examine the fibers with a magnifying glass.

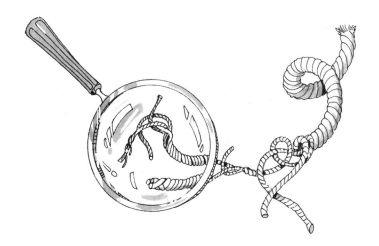

Some will be very smooth and fine. Some will be coarse, with an irregular shape. To compare the strength, pull on the fibers until they break. The properties of the fiber are the basic properties of the rope they become.

Laying a Rope

Many kinds of rope can be cut without unraveling. The twist stays put, so to speak. If you twist two pieces of string together, they untwist themselves as soon as you let go. The art of ropemaking depends on transferring the twist from one place to another. The act of transferring the twist is called "laying" the rope. Here's how to do it.

Materials and Equipment

– three lengths of string or twine two feet long
– scissors
– the back of a chair

Procedure

Tie an end of one length of string around the back of a chair. Tie each of the other two lengths in the same manner, next to the first length. Twist each length in the same direction as its original twist, as tightly as possible. Keep a tight hold to prevent it from untwisting. When a length is tightly twisted, it will twist around itself if you fold it in half. This is the principle of rope-making.

When all three lengths are tightly twisted, hold the ends tightly in one hand. Bring the three tied ends together. Now for the tricky part. You want to cut the ends off the chair without losing your grip and losing the twist. Use the hand that's holding the other ends to do this. The lengths don't have to be held straight. You can bring the hand holding the free ends up to the tied ends, to help out. Just still keep a firm grasp on the free ends so they don't untwist.

Once both twisted ends of all three strands are free, straighten them out so that they lay side by side. Allow them to twist around each other as you let go. The twist you put into each length or strand untwists in such a way that the three strands twist around each other. You can let go of both ends and the twist will not unravel.

Machine-made rope has a much tighter twist than you can put in by hand. Nylon rope will not retain a twist, and the ends easily unravel, so tape is usually put around nylon rope. The ends of polyester rope may be burned to prevent unraveling. Natural fibers, such as cotton, sisal, or jute, will retain the twist to one degree or another. Their ends don't have to be taped.

Observations and Suggestions

Think of the properties needed by cordage doing different kinds of jobs. Rope used on sailboats must remain strong when wet and should resist mildew. Rope used by mountain climbers must stretch so that the rope can absorb some of the shock of a fall, but must also be strong enough not to break under such a shock. Rope for packaging material should be inexpensive. What plant fibers fill the bill? Where are the ropes usually made of synthetic fibers?

Natural Plant Cordage

Most of the cordage you're likely to come across holding packages together will be made of natural plant fibers, as opposed to man-made synthetic fibers. The natural fibers used for cordage are stronger and tougher than fibers used for fabrics, as you might expect. The three natural fibers used most for cordage are Manila hemp (from abaca plants in the Philippine Islands), sisal hemp, and coir. Abaca plants are like banana plants. The fibers are in the stems, which are sometimes fifteen feet long. Sisal fibers are in the sword-shaped leaves in a cactuslike plant. Coir is fiber from the husks of coconuts. Fresh coconuts have had the husks removed before they are brought to a supermarket, but you can pull a few coir fibers off the outside of the shell. Most grocery managers won't mind, if you ask them first.

The natural fibers used for cordage are called "hard" fibers. They are bundles of plant cells that transport water up and down stems or leaves in the living plant. The cells overlap and are bound together by cementing substances produced by the plant. These "bast" fibers, as they are also called, are surrounded by the fleshy cells of the plant. The problem facing the potential rope-maker is to remove the fibers from the surrounding plant material. Do the following to see how this is accomplished.

Materials and Equipment

– fresh pineapple leaves
– scissors
– jar with lid
– hammer
– table knife
– cutting board

Procedure

Pineapple leaves contain bast fibers that are used to make a crisp cottony cloth called piña, and are also twisted into twine for fishing nets. The fibers are not as hard as the bast fibers of Manila hemp or sisal, but you can easily obtain them and experiment with the two basic procedures for removing the fibers from the surrounding fleshy plant material.

You can rot off the fleshy part. This process is called "retting," which is rotting by wetting. Cut the pineapple leaves into lengthwise strips that are about a quarter inch wide. Put them in a jar and cover them with water. Close the lid, and let it sit for a few days. Bacteria on the leaves will become active and the water will become cloudy in a few days. If you take off the lid, you will notice the foul odor of rotting vegetation. Let the leaves sit in the water for about a week. Then rinse them and scrape off the rotten flesh. Piña fibers are white and strong. Retting is also used to remove fibers for hemp and jute.

The other method for removing plant flesh is mechanical and is a much more difficult method for obtaining bast fibers. Hammer the leaves on the cutting board to soften them up. Then scrape away the flesh lengthwise with a blunt table knife. Use a gentle motion with a small amount of pressure. Repeat it, gradually scraping away the flesh. Some bast fibers are produced commercially by a combination of beating and scraping.

Observations and Suggestions

See if you can ret out fibers from other plants. Try banana stems and reeds, for a start.

Fiber Flame Test

You can use a laboratory test to identify different fibers. This test involves a flame, so check with the adult in your house before you attempt to do it.

Materials and Equipment

– samples of different kinds of fibers from all kinds of cordage
– a candle in a candle holder
– matches
– an aluminum-foil pan or ashtray
– tweezers or tongs

Procedure

Hold a frayed end of a sample with the tweezers. Bring the fibers near the flame. Observe its reaction to heat. Briefly put the end of the fibers into the flame and withdraw it immediately. Observe the nature of its burning. Set down the fibers in the foil

Fiber	Approaching flame	In flame	Out of flame	Odor	Ash
cotton sisal hemp coir	does not shrink away from flame	burns	keeps burning	like paper	gray, fine
nylon	fuses and shrinks	burns slowly	goes out	like celery	hard, tough, gray
acetate	fuses away from flame	burns with sparks	keeps burning	like paper and vinegar	hard, black bead
polyester	fuses and shrinks away from flame	burns and melts	usually goes out	like burnt marshmallow	hard bead
fiberglass	does not burn or melt				
linen	does not fuse or shrink	burns, no melting	keeps burning	like cotton	fine gray
silk	fuses and curls away from flame	burns slowly, some melting	burns slowly	like burnt hair	brittle, black bead
wool	fuses and curls away from flame	burns	goes out	like burnt hair	brittle, shiny bead

pan, even if they are still burning. Smell the smoke and observe what's left of the fibers.

Glue

When you put something wet on a dry object, the wet material usually sticks to the dry surface. But if you put two dry objects together, it's most unlikely that they'll stick together. One very important reason is that the two dry objects are not in very close contact with each other. If you could magnify each dry surface to see the molecules, you would find that the surface was far from smooth. The molecules at the surface would be like hills and valleys. When two such surfaces are brought together, the actual points of contact, on the molecular level, are few and far between. Wet materials, on the other hand, can flow and reorganize to fill the irregular spaces of solid materials. Thus they come into much more intimate contact with a solid surface.

If you want to get two dry surfaces to stick together, having something wet between them solves only part of the problem. You need to have a wet material that sticks to itself as well as to the surface, even after the wetness is gone. This is what glues are all about. Most glues are made up of long molecules of repeating units, called polymers. Polymers wrap around each other, giving strength to the dried glue film. When they are wet, glue polymers come in very close contact with surfaces and may interlock with surface molecules. By sticking to a surface and sticking to themselves, glues form adhesive bonds.

Glues form a dry film in making an adhesive bond. You can get a good look at such films in the following experiment.

Materials and Equipment

- plastic wrap
- rubber bands
- jars
- assortment of household glues

Procedure

For each sample of glue, stretch a square of plastic wrap across the mouth of a jar and hold in place with a rubber band. Spread a sample of glue on the stretched surface to make a thin layer about an inch in diameter. Let it dry.

Observations and Suggestions

How is the dry film different in appearance from the wet film? Some glues become clear when they dry. Do a "blush test" to see if they are waterproof. Put a drop of water on the circle of clear dry glue. If it becomes cloudy, the glue is not waterproof.

Does the glue adhere to the plastic? See if you can peel the plastic wrap away from the drop of glue. Glues for porous material probably will not stick. Feel the side of the film that was next to the plastic. Why is it so smooth? Does the glue adhere to metal? Repeat the test, using aluminum foil instead of plastic wrap.

Does glue shrink when it dries? If taut plastic wrap wrinkles, the dried glue does shrink. How can shrinking affect the strength of a bond?

Make Your Own Glue

Historically, glue was made from the skin and hooves of animals.

Such animal-hide glues had to be used when warm. When they cooled they gelled, due to the presence of an animal protein, gelatin. Modern carpenter's glue for wood is a variation of the old animal-hide glues. Chemists have figured out how to keep it flowing when at room temperature. Here's how you can make your own variation of animal glue. It, too, must be spread when warm.

Materials and Equipment

– one package granulated unflavored gelatin
– one tablespoon sugar
– two tablespoons water
– small saucepan with water
– small metal baking cup
– spoon
– potholder or tongs

Procedure

Mix the water, gelatin, and sugar in the small baking cup. Let it stand for a few minutes until all the water is dissolved. Put the cup in the pan of water. Heat it on the stove. Stir the mixture occasionally as the water comes to a boil. Hold the cup with tongs or a potholder. When the water starts to boil, turn off the flame. Keep the mixture over hot water until the gelatin appears to be dissolved.

Try gluing some pieces of paper together. Put a sample on a piece of plastic wrap stretched over a jar. Let it dry so you can see the film you have created. Peel off your film and examine it.

Observations and Suggestions

The sugar acts to slow down the gelling of the gelatin so that it is easier to spread. It is called a *plasticiser* by chemists. Add another tablespoon of sugar to your hot glue mixture. See if it does, in fact, take longer to set. What does a plasticiser do to the flexibility of the glue film?

This formula for glue is not carved in stone. Experiment to see if you can improve upon it.

A good source of gelatin is veal or chicken bones. You can make glue by boiling them in water for at least two hours and then boiling down the strained liquid, letting the water evaporate, until you are left with a thick, gluey mess that gels when cooled.

Tapes

The tapes in your hardware store, from masking tape to electrical tape to decorative tapes to tapes for sealing to reflecting tapes for bikers and joggers, all have one thing in common: they use a pressure-sensitive adhesive. There are a number of pressure-sensitive adhesives around. Some are rubber. Others are synthetic. All of them are tacky to the touch. Here's how you can compare their adhesive strength.

Materials and Equipment

– an assortment of tapes from the hardware store: masking, decorative, electrical, transparent, etc.
– scissors
– blotting paper or cardboard
– metal pie pan

Procedure

Cut three-inch lengths of the different tapes. Press one half of the length onto a piece of paper or cardboard, leaving the other end free. Smooth down the adhered end to make a good, firm bond. Now for the peel test. Fold back the free end of the tape so that it rests back to back with the stuck end. Peel back the adhered end, keeping the tape back to back. Some of the paper fibers will adhere to the peeled tape. The amount of paper fiber sticking to the tape is a measure of the strength of its adhesive bond.

Adhere half of the lengths of the different tapes to a metal pie pan. When you pull them off, you can easily feel the different adhesive strengths of the different tapes.

5. Tools: Simple Machines

An elephant can use its trunk to rip out a tree by its roots. A beaver can chew through a log. A bee can fashion a delicate honeycomb with its mouth parts. By comparison, the human body is distinctly inept. Our only advantage over other creatures is our brain and our hands. But what an advantage! We use our brains and hands to make tools: objects that let us accomplish tasks far beyond the strength, speed, and skillfulness of the human body. We can do wonders with tools, and have. The pyramids of Egypt and the bridges of Rome are called "wonders of the world." They are, in fact, incredible engineering feats built with relatively simple tools and lots of muscle power. These same basic tools have been built into today's heavy construction machinery where fuels supply the power rather than muscle. So although we can be out-pulled or outchewed by other animals, there's no way we're going to be outtooled. Tool-making truly sets us apart.

Think of tools as extensions of human hands and muscles. We use them to increase our ability to strike, turn, cut, and hold. Hand

tools, the kind of devices most people think of when they think of tools, are designed to change the shape of materials and fasten pieces together. A hammer is an extension of a fist; cutting tools extend the ability to tear material apart.

The purpose of tools is to help people do work. Now "work" is one of those words that has one meaning in everyday language and another meaning for scientists. You'll use the word to describe a variety of activities, including sitting at a desk and just thinking. But to a scientist, work is precisely defined so that it can be measured.

To a scientist, work is the movement of materials against some resistance. When you pick up a chair, you do work. The chair is being moved against the resistance of gravity. When you huff and puff and become sweaty trying to lift a grand piano, if the piano is not budged, you do no work in the scientific sense.

There are two parts to scientists' work: force and distance. Force is usually measured in pounds or some other unit of weight. Distance is, of course, measured in either English units (feet, etc.) or metric units (meter, etc.). Work is defined as force times distance. When science makes a term mathematical, it becomes possible to see how to produce the same effect in a variety of ways. Thus you can lift two pounds of material two feet in the air, one pound four feet, or four pounds one foot, and do the same amount of work in each case. You accomplish the same amount of work by moving a lesser force through a larger distance as you do by moving a greater force through a smaller distance.

The different ways the proportions of force and distance can be varied and still produce the same amount of work make tools effective. You do work on a tool. Your force is called *effort.* The tool, in turn, applies your effort to some object or material called the *resistance.* Many tools multiply your effort. In pulling out a nail, you may apply a force of ten pounds to the handle of the hammer. The hammer multiplies your effort by four and applies forty pounds to the nail. The tool has made you four times as strong. This increase in your effort is called the *mechanical advantage* of the tool. There is a trade-off here. You only get a mechanical advantage for increased force by decreasing distance. So in order to pull the nail with a strong force, you pull it a very short distance. Your hand, with the smaller effort, moves through a greater distance.

All lifting tools do work against the resistance of gravity. Friction is another kind of resistance. Some tools, like nails, screws, nuts, and bolts, make friction work for you. Other tools, like saws and files, work against friction as well as against the resistance of the material itself.

You can measure the mechanical advantage of tools. Don't be put off by the math involved. It's easy to see the right way to use tools to give the greatest mechanical advantage. The lawfulness of it all is exciting to discover. Hand tools are variations of devices scientists call *simple machines.* In this chapter, you experiment with tools and discover how they really work.

The Claw Hammer

An animal thigh bone or a rock are good candidates for the first hammer. Our oldest ancestors probably used what they had around and then threw them away when they had finished a task. The Stone Age, which runs from about 6,000 years ago to 2 million years ago, got its name because of its stone tools, which modern archaeologists have discovered. Stone Age people used objects called "pebble tools." They were stones with one rough cutting edge that was used to chop, cut, and scrape. Instead of discarding them, people kept them at hand for daily jobs.

A later ancestor of the hammer was the stone ax, where the cutting head was tied to a wooden handle. In an amazing and mysterious way the addition of the handle multiplied the strength of the arms and let our ancestors cut down trees more easily than they might have dreamed. Building from wood now could become carpentry. The Bronze Age and the Iron Age, which followed, are also named for the materials from which tools were made. Hammers from those periods were an improvement over the stone ax, but not different in principle.

The modern claw hammer is two tools. One end, the claw, is a holding tool. The other end, the face of the hammerhead, is a striking tool for driving nails into wood. As in the case of the ancient stone hammer, the key to the effectiveness of both is the handle. Do an experiment to see how the length of the handle determines the mechanical advantage of the hammer for you.

Materials and Equipment

– a hammer
– three common 4- or 6-penny nails
– a block of wood a little thicker than the length of the nails

Procedure

Tap the nails into the wood about one inch apart so that they stand without being held. Make sure that they all stick out the same distance from the wood.

Hold the hammer by the back of the head. Count how many strokes you need to drive the nail completely into the wood. Hold the hammer in the middle of the handle. Again, count the number of strokes needed to drive in the nail. Finally, hold the hammer at the end of the handle. Again, count the number of strokes needed to drive in the third nail.

Observations and Suggestions

Any carpenter will tell you that you should hold a hammer at the end of the handle when you drive in a nail. How do your results support this idea?

In which case is the hammerhead moving fastest when it strikes the nail? Where does it bounce off the nail head the highest?

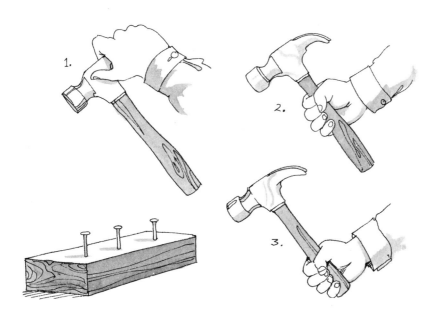

Here's how a hammer works: The force delivered by the face of the head depends on two things: the weight of the hammerhead, and how fast it's moving on impact. Collision with the nail brings the motion of the hammer to a complete stop. The greater the change of speed to zero on impact, the greater the force delivered to the nail. By changing the position of your hand on the handle, you change the speed of the moving head.

A hammer is a variation of a simple machine called a *lever*. The basic lever is a rigid bar that turns on a single point, called the *fulcrum*. The position of the fulcrum, the effort, and the force delivered to the resistance can be changed according to the use of the lever. When you use a hammer to drive a nail, the effort and the fulcrum are in the same place, your hand. The hammerhead delivers the force to the resistance. This kind of arrangement, effort and fulcrum together at one end of the lever, with the resist-

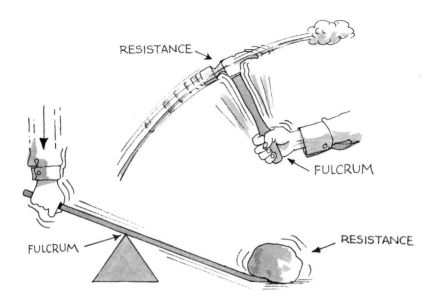

ance force at the other end, gives an increase in speed. The longer the distance between the effort and fulcrum and the resistance, the greater the speed.

There are many variations of this kind of lever. A fishing rod throws the line farther than you could throw it with your arm. A baseball bat drives the ball farther when you hold it at its end and give a full swing. When you choke up on the bat, the ball will never leave the ball park. In fact, your arm is this kind of lever whenever you throw something. Can you now explain why it is more effective to throw with your whole arm rather than flip an object from your elbow?

A hammer can also be used to increase your effort and deliver a greater force to the resistance. You use it this way when you pull out nails. This time the fulcrum is in between the effort and the resistance. The nail is held in the claws, the fulcrum is the back of the hammerhead, and the effort is your hand on the handle.

The distance from the resistance and the fulcrum to your effort and the fulcrum determines how much your effort is multiplied. Check this out. Try and pull out a nail by holding the hammer handle near the hammerhead. Then try by holding it near the end. You'll see that it is much easier to remove the nail when your effort is at the end of the handle.

There are other examples of levers that multiply your effort. When you use a screwdriver to open a can of paint, when you pry off a bottle cap or cut a hole in a can with a can opener, or pry open a crate with a crowbar, you use this type of lever. All of them have the same thing in common: the distance from the resistance to the

fulcrum is much shorter than the distance from your effort to the fulcrum. Work (force times distance) is done at both ends, and the amount of work is equal. When your effort is moved through a larger distance, the resistance is moved through a much smaller distance but with a much greater force.

Calculated Advantages

If you could figure out a way to measure the force you deliver to the handle of the hammer, and the force delivered to the nail you are pulling out, you could figure out the mechanical advantage of the lever. However, there is an easier way. Measure the distance from your hand to the fulcrum. This distance is called the effort arm of the lever. Then measure the distance from the resistance to the fulcrum. This is called the resistance arm of the lever. When you divide the effort arm by the resistance arm, you get the mechanical advantage. The effort arm of my hammer was 11 inches. The resistance arm was 1.5 inches. Here's the formula for the mechanical advantage:

$$\text{Mechanical advantage} = \frac{\text{Effort arm}}{\text{Resistance arm}} = \frac{11''}{1.5''} = 7.3 \ (\text{Mechanical advantage})$$

This means that my effort is multiplied 7.3 times. So if I apply a force of 10 pounds to the hammer, a force of 73 pounds is applied to the nail.

Calculate the mechanical advantages for a can opener and other tools you may have around the house.

A pair of scissors is yet another variation of this kind of lever. If you are cutting some tough material, where is the greatest force delivered, near the fulcrum or near the tips of the blades?

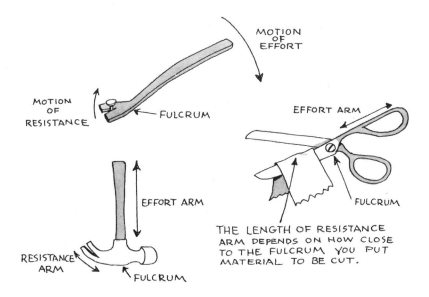

MOTION OF EFFORT

MOTION OF RESISTANCE

FULCRUM

EFFORT ARM

RESISTANCE ARM

FULCRUM

EFFORT ARM

FULCRUM

THE LENGTH OF RESISTANCE ARM DEPENDS ON HOW CLOSE TO THE FULCRUM YOU PUT MATERIAL TO BE CUT.

The Saw

Like the hammer, the saw is also a very old tool. The earliest saws were probably animal jawbones with the teeth attached to be used as saw teeth. The Stone Age saw was a piece of wood studded with tiny points of flint. Naturally, saws made in the Bronze Age and Iron Age were much improved versions. But all the saws are based on the principle of lining up many sharp knives instead of attacking the material with a single blade. Saws were developed in northern countries where there were huge forests. Obviously the people there were interested in tools that improved their ability to work with wood.

There are several different kinds of modern handsaws designed for either cutting or ripping rigid materials. The most obvious difference in the blade of the saw is the number of teeth, or points, per inch. Do an experiment to see the kinds of cuts you can make with a saw with a low point number and a saw with a high point number.

Materials and Equipment

– a small keyhole saw with two blades that fit the same handle (You can buy them for a few dollars at the hardware store, or get a wood saw and a hacksaw.)
– a bright-color crayon
– ruler
– cardboard

Procedure

Start two cuts in one edge of the cardboard by drawing up the blade of the saw two or three times. Measure off a distance on the blade of the saw that is almost its entire length. Mark off the beginning and end of this distance with the crayon. Mark off an equal distance on the second blade. Place the cardboard so that one of the starting grooves is over the edge of a table. Hold it in place. Put the saw tip in the groove so that the surface of the cardboard is even with the mark farthest from the handle. Saw down at about a 45° angle, making a cut, and stop when you reach the second crayon mark on the saw.

Change the blades of the saw. Repeat the procedure with the second blade, in the second groove. Make sure that the second cut is made with the saw held at the same angle as the first one.

Observations and Suggestions

Measure the distance of the cuts. Count the number of points per inch for each blade. I used a saw that had twelve points per inch and a hacksaw blade that had twenty-eight points per inch. The cut made by the first blade was about twice as long as the one made by the second blade. The blade with about twice as many points per inch made a cut half as long. Each blade is suitable for different jobs.

There are different kinds of saws designed to do different kinds of jobs. A crosscut saw has small, even teeth with points that are sharpened like knives. The points bevel in alternate directions, thus giving the effect of two parallel rows of knives. On the downward stroke, which does 75 percent of the cutting (the weight of the sawyer is behind the stroke), the teeth cut the wood in parallel cuts, and the wood in between is crumbled. Crosscut saws work against the grain and have a harder job than saws that cut with the grain. In general, the fewer the teeth per inch, the coarser the cut. Saws with eight points per inch are used to make coarse cuts. Ten and twelve points per inch are used for fine carpentry.

A ripsaw lives up to its name. It rips wood. It is used for cutting with the grain, which offers the least resistance. The large, pointed teeth are slanted forward and hit the wood like a series of chisels, ripping and cutting on the forward motion. Ripsaws are used to cut a board lengthwise.

The hacksaw is used for cutting metal. Since metal offers more resistance than wood, hacksaw blades have more points per inch on average than wood saws. The blades range from fourteen points per inch to thirty-two points per inch. Hacksaws are used for cutting sheet metal as well as metal fasteners like nuts or nails. They've also been used to saw through the bars of a jail. When you cut sheet metal, the general rule is to use finer blades for thinner sheets and coarser blades for thicker sheets. Do an experiment to check this out.

Nails, Tacks, Chisels, and Other Wedges

Nails, tacks, chisels, and knives are all used to penetrate materials. (After penetration, nails and tacks are fasteners using friction to hold things together.) It's no secret that sharp, pointed objects penetrate materials more easily than blunt objects. Think about why this is so. Imagine you are trying to lift a heavy box by sliding a wedge underneath it. The work you are doing is against gravity. The wedge changes the direction of your effort. You push parallel to the floor in the process of raising the edge of the box. The box actually moves up along the slanted surface of the wedge. You gain mechanical advantage by trading off moving your effort through a longer horizontal distance than the vertical distance the resistance is moved. The amount of work you do and the amount that is done on the box is, of course, just about the same.

Nails, tacks, chisels, and knives are all variations on the simple machine known as the wedge. The point of a nail or tack and the blade of a chisel or knife are all wedges. The resistance is the material that they penetrate. The same rule holds true for these instruments as for the wedge used to lift a heavy object: the steeper the wedge, the smaller the mechanical advantage. You might also say that the more gradual the slope, the sharper the blade or point. Do an experiment to check this out.

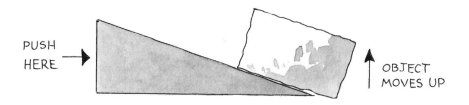

PUSH
HERE

OBJECT
MOVES UP

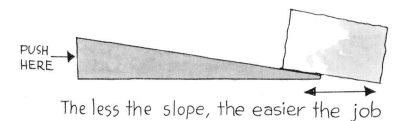

PUSH
HERE

The less the slope, the easier the job

Materials and Equipment

– a collection of nails, tacks, and cutting tools with different steepness to the penetration point
– a metric ruler
– a bar of soap

Procedure

The mechanical advantage of a wedge is its length divided by its widest point. A nail with a point 3 millimeters long and a shaft 1.5 millimeters in diameter has a mechanical advantage of $3/1.5$ or 2. This means that your effort is multiplied by 2 in driving the point into the surface of the resistance.

Measure the lengths and widths (diameter) of your assortment of wedges. (Your measurements will not be exact, but do them as carefully as you can.) Calculate the mechanical advantages for each object. Now gently rest the point of an object on the surface of a bar of soap. See how hard you have to push to get the point to penetrate the resistance. Compare the different objects, checking only the sharpness of the points. The larger the diameter of a nail, the more effort is needed for penetration. This factor must be considered when you compare wedges. Once you penetrate past the point, the diameter of the nail will affect the force you need for penetration.

Observations and Suggestions

How does sharpening a cutting tool increase its mechanical advantage? What does the steepness of a ramp tell you about the effort needed to reach the top?

Screws

The invention of the screw is credited to Archimedes, a famous Greek mathematician and inventor who lived 250 years before Christ. His screw was used to raise water from rivers and streams to irrigate fields. It was made of wood and enclosed in a wooden cylinder. When the screw was turned, water climbed the "spiral staircase."

Modern screws are found doing all sorts of jobs, including holding pieces of wood together. You can also find screws at work in meat grinders, vises, and cider presses, to name a few examples.

A screw is a ramp, or kind of wedge, wrapped around a cylinder. The surface of the ramp makes up the threads of a screw. Each complete turn of a screw drives it the distance between two threads.

There are several advantages screws have over nails. They provide more holding power because the threads increase the surface contact between the screw and the material. They can be easily removed without damaging the material, except for the hole they made. They require less force to insert.

Do an experiment to get a feel for the mechanical advantage of screws.

Materials and Equipment

– a bar of soap
– common nails with diameters equal to the screws you use
– a variety of wood and sheet-metal screws of different   diameters
– measuring tape

Procedure

Push a nail into the bar of soap. Now screw in a screw of equal diameter. You don't need a screwdriver. Just hold the screw between your index finger and thumb, and twirl it clockwise. It will cut its way into the soap. Compare screws of different diameters.

Screw diameters are measured by gauge number. The most common are numbers 2 through 16. Screw length is measured in inches. Nail sizes are in penny rating. At one time the penny rating was the price per 100 nails. The abbreviation "d" comes from the word "denarius," an early Roman coin. Today, the penny rating refers to the overall length and diameter of a nail.

Observations and Suggestions

You can calculate the mechanical advantage of a screw. The mechanical advantage is the ratio between the distance you move your effort, or the circumference of the shaft of the screw, and the distance moved through the resistance, or the distance between threads.

This can be expressed mathematically:

$$\text{Mechanical advantage} = \frac{\text{Circumference (pi} \times \text{diameter)}}{\text{Distance between threads (1/pitch)}}$$

You can figure out the distance between threads by counting the number of threads in an inch or *pitch*. If there are sixteen threads in one inch, the pitch is sixteen and the distance between threads is 1/16 of an inch.

A #4 screw has a diameter of .112 inches. Its pitch is 16 threads per inch. The distance between threads is 1/16 inch, or 0.06 inch. Plugging in the numbers in to the formula, you get:

$$\text{Mechanical advantage} = \frac{.112 \times 3.14}{.06} = 5.86$$

The screw multiplies your force more than five times.

You might like to calculate the mechanical advantage for screws of other diameters. Here's a table for different screw numbers and their diameters. Figure 16 threads per inch as the usual pitch, or .06 inch as the distance between threads:

Screw #	1	2	3	4	5	6	7	8
Diameter	.073	.086	.099	.112	.125	.138	.151	.164

What happens to the mechanical advantage as the diameter of the screw increases? How do your calculations compare with the force you felt with your fingers screwing different-size screws into the soap?

Turning Tools

When you use a lever, your effort moves on a straight line and the resistance is moved on a straight line. There is a class of tools where your effort moves through a large circle and the resistance through a very small circle. If you imagine your effort as the path made by the rim of an imaginary wheel, the path of the resistance is its axle. For this reason, tools that give a gain in force through circular motion are variations on the simple machine called the "wheel and axle." Wrenches and screwdrivers are examples. Get a feeling for their mechanical advantage.

Materials and Equipment

– two screwdrivers, one large and one small
– ruler, pencil and paper

– two identical wood screws numbered 3, 4, or 5
– block of soft wood
– awl, or nail and hammer

Procedure

Measure the diameter of each screwdriver handle. Measure the width of the blade tip. Write down your measurements.

Use the awl or the nail and hammer to make starting holes in the wood about an inch apart. Screw in one screw with the large screwdriver, and one with the small. Which screw went in more easily? If you aren't certain, screw in a few more with each screwdriver.

Observations and Suggestions

The ratio between the distance your effort moves (the circumference of the wheel) and the distance the resistance moves (the circumference of the axle) is the mechanical advantage.

As with other simple machines, the number of times your effort is multiplied depends on the ratio between the distance your effort moves and the distance the resistance moves. In this case, your effort moves through the circumference of the screwdriver handle (circumference = pi × diameter), and your resistance moves through the circumference of the tip of the blade of the screwdriver. This can be expressed mathematically:

$$\text{Mechanical advantage} = \frac{\text{Diameter of handle} \times \text{pi}}{\text{Width of the blade} \times \text{pi}}$$

Pi is eliminated as a factor because it appears in both the numerator and denominator.

A screwdriver with a handle diameter of 1 inch and a blade diameter of ¼ inch has a mechanical advantage of 4. (M.A. = 1/¼

= 4.) Thus, if you apply a force of 5 pounds to the handle, a force of 20 pounds is applied to the screw.

Wrenches also work on this principal. One end of a wrench grips an object, the other is the handle where force is applied. Where should you hold a wrench for maximum mechanical advantage, in the center of the handle or near its end? Do an experiment to check out your guess.

Look for simple wheel-and-axle machines around your house. Doorknobs, keys, and can openers are good ones for a start. Measure their mechanical advantages.

6. Electricity

When electrical problems strike, the hardware store can come to the rescue. Wires, switches, batteries, plugs, sockets, and fuses are familiar stuff to the do-it-yourselfers. Why hire someone to rewire a lamp or change a plug when the task is basically quite simple? There are some underlying principles behind electricity, and when you understand them, there is almost no limit to the use you can put them to.

Electricity is a form of energy. Like light and heat and sound, electricity can be found free in nature. From the giant sparks of lightning in the summer sky to your sweater sticking to your shirt or your hair standing on end when you comb it on a cold day, this electricity, called *static* electricity, is not serving any useful purpose. You can't run a television or a toaster or a light bulb on static electricity.

But what you can do is study it. For thousands of years no one

66

knew how. Static electricity was a fascinating oddity, like the lodestone, a rock that attracted metal objects that stuck to it. Then, about 250 years ago, scientists went to work on the problems of electricity and magnetism. These scientists were interested only in producing truth about nature. They had no idea where these truths might lead. But once there was some truth, ahhh . . . inventors' imaginations caught fire. Scientific truth put to work became technology. Static electricity was no longer the only electrical game in town. Electricity now was a current flowing through wires, energy moving steadily from one place to another. And when you've got that kind of harness on energy, well, let's say the world was electrified with countless applications.

The experiments in this chapter will introduce you to electricity. I think you'll get a charge out of them!

Charges

Begin your study of electricity by checking out the natural phenomenon of static electricity just as early scientists did. The ancient Greeks discovered a peculiar event that occurred when amber, a petrified resin they called "elektron," was rubbed. Rubbed amber attracted threads and feathers and bits of fluff through space. Rubbed amber now had what is called a "charge." You can produce an electrical charge by rubbing lots of different things. Collect as much of the following as possible.

Materials and Equipment

– items made of the following materials: plastic (a comb), rubber (a comb), glass (a drink stirring rod works best), wool, silk, newspaper, pencil, fabrics from the dryer such as nylon, dacron, polyester

Procedure

Rub the different items with the different fabrics. Rub plastic and rubber with wool, glass with silk, newspaper with the pencil. Rub an inflated balloon on your hair.

See if you have a charge. Pass the rubbed object over tiny bits of torn-up paper, or pass it over your arm and see if your hairs feel it. Or see if it sticks to the wall.

Touch a charged object. What happens to the charge?

Bring two charged objects together. When the charged objects are the same, what happens? Bring two different charged objects together. Make a record of what happens each time.

Observations and Suggestions

You will find that at times two charged objects will move toward each other. At other times, two charged objects will move away from each other. Objects that move away from each other have the same charge. Objects that move toward each other have the opposite charge. The rule is: "Like charges repel, opposites attract."

The dryer is a good place to find charged materials. See what charge is carried by different fabrics coming out of the dryer. They will have either the charge of a rubbed balloon or of a rubbed glass.

When you touch a charged object, the charge disappears. This is called *grounding.* The electricity moves into other materials (the ground) and is no longer concentrated in the rubbed object.

Make a Charge Detector

An electroscope is a device that detects and measures the strength of static electricity. An electroscope has two easily charged objects, called leaves, hanging from a metal hook. An electroscope detects a charge when the leaves move apart. They move apart because they each have the same charge, and like charges repel. Electroscope leaves can detect both kinds of charges, called *positive* or *negative*. There are several kinds of electroscopes you can make, and you might want to try making them all to see which one works best for you.

Materials and Equipment

Electroscope #1:
- paper clip or safety pin
- cork, or small piece of cardboard three or four folds thick
- silk thread
- balls of puffed rice, popcorn, styrofoam, or any other kind of lightweight nonmetal

Electroscope #2:
- paper clip or safety pin
- cork or cardboard
- Christmas tree tinsel

Electroscope #3:
- paper clip or safety pin
- cork or cardboard
- tissue paper
- aluminum paint in a spray can

Assemble your electroscopes as shown in the diagrams:

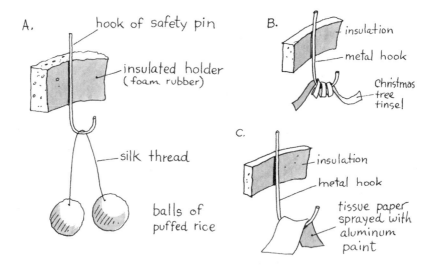

A. hook of safety pin
insulated holder (foam rubber)
silk thread
balls of puffed rice

B. insulation
metal hook
Christmas tree tinsel

C. insulation
metal hook
tissue paper sprayed with aluminum paint

To use your electroscope:

Hold your electroscope by the cork or the cardboard. Bring charged objects near the leaves of your electroscope. As the charged object approaches, the leaves separate. Move your charged object away. Watch what happens to the leaves.

Bring your charged object near the end of the metal clip or safety pin that's sticking through the holder. This is called the *electrode.* Do the leaves become charged? If they do, the charge is being *conducted* to the leaves through the metal wire. Metals are electrical *conductors.* The motion of electricity through a conductor is called a *current.* Nonmetals that you've been experimenting with do not conduct electricity. An electric charge stays put until it leaks into the air or is grounded. It is called *static* electricity because it doesn't move. What happens when you take your charged object away from the electrode? Do the leaves keep the charge?

What happens when you touch your charged object quickly to an electrode and then remove it?

What happens when you bring other charged objects near charged electroscope leaves?

Observations and Suggestions

A charged object acts through space to cause a temporary charge on the electroscope leaves. This influence through a distance is called *induction*. You induce a charge when you bring a charged object near, but not touching, the electroscope leaves or electrode. As soon as you remove the influence of the charged object, the induced charge disappears. Charged objects stick to other objects because they induce the opposite charge in the other material, and opposite charges attract each other. They stick to each other until the charge leaks away.

The leaves remain open after the electrode has been touched by a charged object. The electrode grounds the object (removes its charge) and conducts the electricity to the leaves, which now remain apart. Electricity will always move toward a conductor if it gets the chance. This is the principle of the lightning rod. A piece of metal in a high place that is long enough to go into the ground will attract lightning and conduct its charge harmlessly into the ground.

Charged electroscope leaves will open farther or collapse when other charged objects approach. They open farther if the approaching charged object has the same charge, and collapse when it has the opposite charge.

You may notice that some objects have a stronger charge than others. Some electroscope leaves will retain a charge longer than others, as well. If you spray the puffed rice or popcorn in the first electroscope with aluminum paint, it may retain a charge longer. Humidity will have a large effect on static electricity. Your experiments will work best on a cold, dry day. You may be quite frustrated getting results on a hot, muggy one. That's because moisture in the air "grounds" charges easily.

Make a Current Detector

It's now time to get a little theory behind electricity. The theory is based on experimental work of chemists as well as physicists studying electricity and heat. It focuses on the modern concept of the smallest particles of matter, the atom. No one has ever seen an atom, it is so small. But lots and lots of experimental evidence, such as tracks in a cloud chamber made by moving atoms or their parts, has enabled scientists to create a working model of an atom that accounts for the evidence. So we'll jump way ahead of the story that starts with a study of static electricity, and take a brief look at electrical theory.

As small as an atom is, it is made of even smaller particles that are arranged around each other like miniature solar systems. An atom has a nucleus, like the sun, that bears a positive electrical charge. Tiny particles, called *electrons,* whirl about the nucleus like miniature planets. Electrons are negatively charged. Electrons are the currency of electricity. They are able to move from one atom to another. In an uncharged atom, the total negative charge due to the orbiting electrons is equal to the total positive charge of the nucleus. But when electrons move to other atoms and the distribution becomes uneven, electricity is the result. When you rub a material to create a static charge, you are rubbing electrons from one material to another. The material that gets extra electrons is now more negative, and the material that loses electrons becomes positive. Grounding allows the balance to be restored, as the ground has an almost limitless supply of electrons or positively charged particles to take up extra electrons and neutralize any imbalance.

The electrons of metal atoms move very easily from one atom to another. Thus, metals conduct a flow of electrons in a manner similar to water flowing through pipes. Such an electrical current is created when extra electrons (negatively charged) are pushed into one end of the conductor when they move toward the other end (the positively charged electrode).

A device that detects an electric current is called a *galvanometer.* You can make a simple galvanometer quite easily and use it for lots of experiments.

Materials and Equipment

– an inexpensive compass
– ten feet of bell wire (get at a hardware store)
– cardboard
– scissors

Procedure

Cut the cardboard into a rectangle that can form a cradle for the compass, with the ends bent up as shown. Set the compass so that the north-south poles as written on the dial face the cardboard sides. Hold the compass in place by winding the bell wire around the cardboard holder in the same direction as the north-south compass axis. Make your coil as compact as possible. It will have about twenty-five turns. Flatten the bottom wire so the compass will rest horizontally and the needle can rotate freely. Leave both ends of wire free. They should be about three inches long.

Now strip the insulation off the ends of the wires to bare the copper. To do this, cut through the insulation but be careful not to cut through the wire, with the scissors about half an inch from the end. When the cut is complete all the way around the insulation, the insulation sleeve will pull off easily.

To use your galvanometer, set it on the table and make sure it is level so that the needle can swing freely. Turn it so that the needle hovers over the north-south axis, parallel to the wires. Test your galvanometer with a flashlight battery as a source of electrical current. Put one bare wire on one electrode of the battery and the other bare wire on the opposite electrode. If the battery is not dead, the needle of the compass will move in an east-west direction. If the current is strong, the needle will spin on its pivot.

Save your galvanometer for the next experiments.

Observations and Suggestions

A galvanometer nicely demonstrates the relationship between magnetism and electricity. A magnet is a piece of metal that attracts other magnets and pieces of iron through a distance. This attraction is similar to the attraction of static electricity. The space surrounding a magnet, through which it exerts its influence, is called its *magnetic field*. On a bar magnet the field is strongest at each end, or at the *poles*. If you fool around with two bar magnets, you'll see that two of the poles will repel each other, and two will attract each other strongly. Again, as in static electricity, like repels and opposites attract.

The earth itself is a magnet. If a bar magnet is allowed to swing freely from one point on its center, one end will point toward the earth's north pole and the other will point toward the earth's south pole. A compass needle is simply a magnet, free to rotate to come to rest in a north-south direction, lining up with the earth's magnetic field.

When a current runs through a wire, it sets up a magnetic field around the wire. A coil of wire strengthens this field in your galvanometer. A current may set up a field that is stronger than the pull of the earth's poles. The compass needle now swings in an east-west direction. If the current is strong enough, the compass needle will spin rapidly.

Batteries

A battery is a source of stored electricity for a variety of uses. It makes an electric current through a chemical reaction. This

reaction causes one electrode in the battery to lose electrons and the other to gain electrons. Electrons move from one electrode to the other through the substance between them. This substance is called an electrolyte. It may be either an acid or an alkaline. In a wet cell that you make, it will be a solution. In a dry cell battery, the electrolyte isn't really dry. Moist, solid chemicals are used instead of a solution.

Here's how to make your own wet-cell battery.

Materials and Equipment

– *Positive electrode:* carbon or copper.

Use a stick of compressed charcoal (from an art supply store or stationery store).

Get three feet of bare copper wire (hardware store). Fold it in half, in half again, and in half again. Twist the strands tightly together.

– *Negative electrode:* Use a zinc mason-jar cover (from a hardware store or houseware department). Hammer the glass insert carefully so it breaks and you can remove it. Hammer it flat. Use a nail to punch a hole in one end for a wire lead.

– *Electrolytes:* sal ammonium or ammonium chloride. (One source said that sal ammonium could be obtained at the hardware store. It is a block used for cleaning solder off soldering irons. I couldn't find it. But if you do and want to try it, smash a small block into powder so that it dissolves more readily. I did get ammonium chloride from a local drugstore. You need about four ounces. The druggist didn't even charge me!)

Other possible electrolytes: distilled vinegar, household ammonia.

– large, open-mouth quart jar
– bell wire
– galvanometer
– scissors
– electrical tape (optional)

Procedure

First prepare your electrodes. Cut two lengths of bell wire about eight inches long. Strip about two inches of insulation off one end and a half inch off the other end of each piece. Put the longer lead through the hole in the zinc piece, and twist the end around the wire. Make sure there is plenty of contact between the copper wire and the zinc. Hold it in place with a piece of electrical tape. Wrap the longer lead of the other wire around the piece of charcoal. Hold it in place with tape.

Fill the jar up to one inch below the brim with water. Stir in the ammonium chloride. Hang the zinc electrode on one side of the jar completely submerged in the electrolyte solution, and hang the charcoal from the other side. They must not be touching.

Connect the lead from one electrode to a lead from your galvanometer. Touch the leads from the other electrode to the remaining lead from the galvanometer. If your battery is generating electricity, the compass needle will move from its north-south position the instant contact is made.

Observations and Suggestions

When you connect the leaders from the electrodes of your wet cell to the galvanometer, you are forming an electric circuit. The extra electrons that have been built up on the zinc now flow through the wire, around the coil over the compass, and back to the carbon electrode, which has a shortage of electrons. When you separate the wires so they don't make contact, you break the circuit.

See if you can generate a current with other types of electrodes and electrolytes. You may be able to get bare zinc wire from your hardware store. Twist a length of it as you twisted the copper wire, to make an electrode. See if a lemon can serve as an electrolyte. Roll a lemon under your foot on the floor so the internal structure breaks down and the juice can flow more freely. Make two insertions on either side of the lemon with a slim knife. Stick a zinc electrode in one slit and the copper one in the other. Do you get a current?

Circuits

The positive and negative electrodes of a battery are a source of electric current as soon as they are connected to each other. Such a connection is called an electric circuit. When other devices, such as a light bulb, are included in the circuit, the electric current can be put to work. Otherwise, a current just running through the battery will quickly waste the electricity, leaving you with a dead battery.

The strength of a circuit depends on the volts in the batteries. A volt is a measure of electrical pressure, or the electrical force pushing through the wires. Flashlight batteries and an ordinary dry cell may have only 1½ volts. Such low voltage can only push electricity through small circuits. Your outlets in your home are 120 volts. This is high enough to complete most of the circuits in your home, and can also give you a nasty shock. Think of voltage as if it were water pressure coming out of a hose. High water pressure will send the water much farther than low water pressure.

Do an open-ended experiment to explore various aspects of an electric circuit.

Materials and Equipment

– a six-volt lantern battery
– bell wire
– scissors
– electrical tape
– a six-volt flashlight bulb in a miniature ceramic socket
– screwdriver
– Optional equipment for further experimentation:
– knife switch
– a glass of salt water
– a nail file
– aluminum foil
– lead for a mechanical pencil

Procedure

Here's how to set up your basic circuit. Cut two lengths of bell wire about eight inches long. Strip the insulation off each end, leaving leads of about half an inch of bare wire. Connect one end of each wire to the positive and negative terminals (electrodes) of the battery. Tape them in place with electrical tape. Unscrew one of the screws on the side of the light socket. Wind a wire lead from one of the battery terminals around the screw. Tighten the screw. Insert the bulb into the socket. To complete the circuit, touch the bare lead of the wire coming from the other battery terminal to the other screw of the light socket. The bulb will light up the instant the circuit is complete.

Add a switch to the circuit, if you wish. Cut another length of wire and strip the ends. Attach one end to the unattached screw of the light socket and attach the other end to one of the screws at the base of a small knife switch. Leaving the switch in the open position, attach the lead from the unconnected battery terminal to the unattached screw of the knife switch. When you close the switch, contact is made among electrical conductors and the circuit is complete.

You can use bare wire leads of your circuit with the light bulb to check various materials around the house to see if they are electrical conductors. Touch bare leads to aluminum foil, metal tools, lead for a mechanical pencil, wood, paper, etc. The bulb will tell you what's what.

See an electrolyte in action. Cut two one-inch squares of aluminum foil. Fold each in quarters, and stick a bare lead into each square so that the wire is surrounded by foil. Hold it in place with electrical tape. Put each of these electrodes in a glass of salt water. Is the circuit completed?

Salt is known as a strong electrolyte. Here are some other electrolytes you may have around your house: vinegar, baking soda (in solution), lemon juice, orange juice, soda water. Most of them are weaker than salt, and the bulb may not light up.

A short circuit is a break in the circuit that is so small that the electricity jumps across the gap. This produces a spark, which can cause a fire. You can produce a short circuit repeatedly and quite safely by making a "sparkler" with a nail file. This will run down your battery, so you won't want to do too much of it. Disconnect the lead to the socket. Wrap one end of a lead from one terminal around the handle of a metal nail file. Run the bare wire coming from the other terminal up and down the rough part of the file. You will see tiny sparks coming from the wire. Do this in the dark to see them better. These tiny sparks are arcs of light, similar to lightning, caused by electricity passing through the air. The bumps on the nail file constantly short the circuit, causing the spaces the sparks jump across. You will feel the nail file getting warm as you do this, which is a sign to stop.

Observations and Suggestions

You can get a real appreciation for the speed of an electric current. Do you notice any time lapse between the completion of the circuit and the bulb's lighting up? Electricity travels almost at the speed of light, which is 186,000 miles per second—instantaneous for the short distance it travels in your circuits.

Resistance

There are a number of materials that will conduct an electric current under certain circumstances, when the voltage is high enough. These materials offer *resistance* to a current. Such resistance can be put to good use. Explore electrical resistance in the next activity.

Materials and Equipment

– a six-volt lantern battery
– bell wire
– scissors
– electrical tape
– piece of lead for a mechanical pencil

– one foot of thin, bare picture wire or other thin wire
– light bulb in miniature socket

Procedure

One obvious result of electrical resistance is heat. Even in good conductors there is some resistance to an electrical current and the wires grow warm, if not hot. Some wires can get hot enough to glow and emit light. This is the principle of the incandescent light bulb. You can see a wire glow red hot. Cut off an eight-inch piece of bare wire. Leave a two-inch end, and wrap the middle six inches around a piece of bell wire, forming a tiny coil. Leave two inches at the other end. Pull the wire off the bell wire. Strip the ends two 3 inch lengths of bell wire so that there is a half inch of bare wire at each end for connections. Attach one end of each bell wire to each end of your resistance wire, and put electrical tape around the connections. Attach one lead of one bell wire to a terminal of the battery.

BEFORE YOU DO THE NEXT STEP, CHECK WITH AN ADULT. THE RESISTANCE WIRE WILL BE RED HOT. Hold the resistance wire in the air by the insulated bell wire. Do not touch the resistance wire! Make a hook out of the remaining bare lead. Hook it into the other terminal. Watch as your "filament" glows.

A material resistant to a flow of electrons can be used to vary the amount of current. Mount a piece of lead from a mechanical pencil on a small piece of cardboard by taping down the ends. Make a circuit from your battery as follows: Connect one terminal to a miniature socket with a bulb. Connect a free lead from the other terminal on the socket. Connect a second free lead to the other battery terminal. Tape one free lead to one end of the pencil lead. Touch the other free lead to the pencil lead to complete the circuit. Move it up and down the lead. Watch as the light brightens and dims as your probe moves.

Observations and Suggestions

The electric light bulb is considered by many to be Thomas Edison's (1847–1931) most important invention. It certainly had a lot of competition, for Edison held 1300 patents by the time he died. Among his favorites were the phonograph, the motion picture, wax paper, and the mimeograph machine. But the electric light bulb was, perhaps, his greatest challenge. The problem that faced him was to find a filament that would glow white hot for a long enough period of time for it to be useful for illumination. He tested thousands of different filaments in glass bulbs from which he had removed all the air. The bulb had to contain a vacuum because the presence of oxygen would cause the glowing wire to simply burn up. Edison and his staff in his laboratory worked on the problem for almost two years and spent over $50,000 in the effort before they found what they were looking for, in 1879. Edison made a bulb with a filament of charred cotton thread. When a current was passed through it in a vacuum bulb, it glowed white hot for forty hours without melting, evaporating, or breaking.

The charred thread consisted of carbon. Carbon will conduct electricity with great resistance. In your second experiment with the lead, you are actually using the resistance of carbon to regulate the flow of electrons. Pencil lead is really graphite, a form of carbon. The distance the electricity has to flow along the graphite rod determines the resistance. You may have noticed that the light was dimmest when the wire leads were as far apart as possible.

The heat of an exposed wire can easily start a fire if it comes in contact with flammable material. A fuse is a protection against such a short circuit. It "blows" when more current is going through a wire than it can normally carry without overheating. The important part of a fuse is a piece of resistant material that becomes a part of a circuit when the fuse is in place. When the circuit is overloaded, and there is too much current being used, the resistant wire gets hot. When it gets hot enough, a weak area melts through and breaks. This breaks the circuit. The electricity may go off, but no fires will start.

You may wish to check the wiring of various electrical items in your home. Look for frayed or missing insulation, especially near plugs and where the wires attach to the appliance or lamp. If you find poor wires, don't use the item. A salesperson at your hardware store will explain how you can fix it.

Index

abaca plants, 36

abrasives, for cleaning surfaces, 4, 10, 11

acids, as cleaners, 12, 16

adhesives, 40, 44
  see also glues; tapes

alcohol, 23

aluminum, 12–13, 16, 17

amber, 67

ammonia, 16–17
  as fixative, 16

animal bones, *see* bones, animal

animal glue, 41–42

Archimedes, 60

atoms, 72–73

ax, stone, 49

bacteria, 37

baseball bats, 52

bast fibers, 36–38

batteries, 75–78

beeswax, 17, 20

binders, 25, 28–29, 30

blades, 55–58

blush test, 41

bones, animal
  gelatin from, 44
  as hammers, 49
  as saws, 55

brass, 16

Bronze Age, 49, 55

can openers, 53

carbon (*cont.*)
  as black pigment, 28
  as conductor, 83
carnauba wax, 20
casein paint, recipe for, 30
chalks, 28
charcoal, as black pigment, 28
charge, electrical, 67–73
chemical reactions
  of aluminum vs. silver, 12
  in batteries, 75–78
  of drying oils, 27
  in metal tarnish, 5, 11–13
  in photography, 13–16
chemicals
  for cleaning, 4
  as electrolytes, 76–78
chisels, 58–60
chlorine, 15
circuits, 77–81, 82
  short, 80–81, 84
claw hammers, 49–54
cleaners, 4–10
  in colonial America, 4
  hard-surface, 6–7, 8, 10
  for metals, 10–13, 16–17
  wetting agents and, 8–10
coconuts, fibers from, 36
coins
  British, 10
  Roman, 62
coir, 36
compasses, 73–74, 75
conductors, electrical, 70, 80, 81–84
copper, 10, 16

cordage, 31–38
  natural plant, 36–38
  types of, 31–32
crosscut saws, 57
crowbars, 53
current, 67, 70, 75–78, 83
  detection of, 72–75
  resistance to, 81–84
  speed of, 81
cutting tools, 47, 54–60

Daguerre, Louis, 13
denarius, 62
detergent, 6–7
distance, 48, 53–54, 62
dry cell batteries, 76
drying oils, 25–27
dyes, 22

Edison, Thomas, 83
effort, tools and, 48, 51–54, 58–65
egg tempera, recipe for, 30
electricity, 12, 13, 66–84
  circuits and, 77–81
  measurement of, 78
  resistance and, 81–84
  speed of, 81
  static, 66–72
  storage of, 75–78
electrodes, 70–71, 76–78
electrolytes, 13, 76–78, 80
electrons, 72–73, 77–78, 82–83
electroscopes, 69–72
"elektron," 67
emulsion, 6–7, 10

evaporation, solvents and, 22, 23
experiments
    with adhesive strengths, 44–45
    with circuits, 79–81
    with drying of oils, 26–27
    with electrical charges, 67–68
    with electrical resistance, 81–84
    with electroscopes, 69–72
    with fiber flame test, 38–39
    with galvanometers, 73–75
    with glue films, 41
    with glue making, 42–44
    with hammers, 50
    with hard-surface cleaners, 6–7
    with laying rope, 34–36
    with metal tarnish, 11–13
    with paint films, 24–25
    with paint making, 28–30
    with photochemistry, 13–16
    with pigments, 27–28
    with plant fibers, 37–38
    with saws, 56–57
    with screws, 61–63
    with wax melting points, 18–20
    with wedges, 59–60
    with wet-cell batteries, 76–78
    with wetting agents, 8–10
    with wheel and axle tools, 63–65
extender pigments, 28

fat, in soap, 6
fibers, 31, 33–34
    flame test for, 38–39
    types and sources of, 36–38

filaments, 82–83
fixatives, 16
flame test for fibers, 38–39
flax plants, 26–27
flint, 55
force, 48, 51–54, 61
    measurement of, 54
friction, 48–49, 58
fulcrums, 51–54
fuses, 84

galvanometers, 73–75, 77–78
gelatin, 42–44
glues, 32, 40–44
    animal, 41–42
graphite, 83
gravity, resistance of, 47, 48, 58
grease, 6
Greeks, ancient, 60, 67
grounding, 68, 71, 72, 73

hacksaws, 57
hammers, 49–55
handles, strength multiplied by, 49–54
handsaws, 55–58
hard fibers, 36–38
hardware, early types of, 1
heat, electricity and, 81–84
honeycombs, 20
"hot-water bath," 19

induction, 71

iodine, in photochemistry, 13–16
ions, silver vs. aluminum, 13
Iron Age, 49, 55

knives, 55, 58–60

lampblack, 28
lasso, 33
latex paints, 23
levers, 51–54, 63
light, 82, 83
    in photochemical reactions, 13–16
    speed of, 81
light bulbs, 78–81, 83
lightning rods, 71
linen, 27
linseed oil, 26–27
liquids, surface tension of, 8
lodestone, 67

magnetism, 74–75
Manila hemp, 36, 37
mechanical advantage, 48–49, 54,
    58–60, 61–65
    ratios for, 54, 62–63, 64
melting points, 18–20
mercury, 13
metal surfaces, cleaners for, 10–13,
    16–17
metal tarnish, 5, 10–13, 16–17
molecules
    of binders, 25
    in emulsion, 6
    of linseed oil, 27
    of paint films, 23

of surfaces, 40
surface tension of, 8
of waxes, 17
mortar and pestle, 28
mumiya, 17
mummies, 1, 17

nail files, "sparklers" made with,
    80–81
nails, 48, 50–54, 58–60
    in frontier America, 1
    penny ratings of, 62
    screws vs., 61, 62
natural plant fibers, 31, 36–39
Niepce, Joseph, 13
nondrying oils, 25–26
nucleus, 72
nylon rope, 35

oil-based paints, 23
    recipe for, 29–30
oils
    drying, 25–27
    varieties of, 25–27
opaqueness, 27

paints, 21–30
    definition of, 21
    films of, 23–25
    "mummy" shade of, 1
    recipes for, 29–30
    three ingredients of, 22
    types of, 21, 23, 29–30
paraffin wax, 20
pebble tools, 49

pencil lead, 82–83
pewter, 16, 17
photochemistry, 13–16
photography, beginnings of, 13, 15, 16
pigments, 22, 27–30
    types and sources of, 28
piña, 37
pineapples, fibers from, 37
pitch, of screws, 62–63
plant fibers, 31, 36–39
plant waxes, 17–18
plasticisers, 43
plies of ropes, 33
poles, 74–75
polishes, 5
    homemade, 16–17
polyester rope, 35
polymers, 25, 40
pressure-sensitive adhesives, 32, 44–45
pumice, 4

ramps, 60
resistance, electrical, 81–84
resistance, mechanical, 47–49, 51–54, 62
    of metal vs. wood, 57
    of wedges, 58–60
retting, 37–38
ripsaws, 57
ropes, 33–37
    anatomy of, 33–34
    early uses of, 33
    laying of, 34–36

twist in, 33–35
    types of, 35
rottenstone, 4

sand, as cleaner, 4
saws, 55–58
    types of, 57–58
scissors, 54
screwdrivers, 53, 64–65
screws, 60–63
    gauge numbers of, 62
semidrying oils, 25–26
shellac, 23
shocks, electric, 78
short circuit, 80–81
silver, 10–12
    in photochemistry, 13–16
    sterling, 10
    tarnishing of, 11–12
simple machines, 46–65
sisal hemp, 36, 37
slope, 58–60
soaps, 4
    types of, 6–7
sockets, 79–81
solvents, 21, 22, 23, 27
sparks, 80–81
speed, changes in, 51, 52
static electricity, 66–72
sterling, 10
Stone Age, 49, 55
stone tools, 49–50
sulfur in tarnish, 11–13
surface tension, 8, 17
surfactants, 8, 9, 10

switches, 80

tacks, 58–60
tapes, 32, 44–45
tarnish, 10–13, 16–17
tempera, egg, 30
thinners, 22
tin, 16, 17
tools, 46–65
    cutting type of, 55–58
    lever type of, 49–54
    wedge type of, 58–63
    wheel and axle type of, 63–65
turpentine, 27
twist
    direction names for, 33
    in rope, 33–35

universal solvent, 6

vacuum, in light bulbs, 83
vehicles, for paints, 22

viscosity, 25
voltage, 78–79

water, as universal solvent, 6
waxes, 17–20
    definition of, 17
    properties of, 5, 17–18
    purity of, 18–20
    types and sources of, 17, 20
wedges, 58–60
wet-cell batteries, 76–78
wet plates, 16
wetting agents, 8–10
wheel and axle tools, 63–65
wire coils, 73–75, 82
wiring, 84
wood, 55, 57
Worcestershire sauce, 17
work
    hammers and, 51–54
    scientific definition of, 47–49
    wedges and, 58–60
wrenches, 65